Powered by GOATA: Move Like the Greatest Of All Time Athletes

Jose G Boesch

Copyright © 2019 Jose G Boesch

Text Reid Singer, on behalf of Story Terrace

Cover Carly Langford

Edited by Todd M Sisung and Gavin W Boesch

All rights reserved.

ISBN: 978-1-0777-2291-0

CONTENTS

1	How The GOATA System Was Born	1
2	Pre-Movement Fundamentals	Pg 14
3	Training To Perfect GOATA Movement	Pg 41
4	In The Studio	Pg 56
5	Drills And Exercises For GOATA Strength	Pg 67
6	Drills And Exercises For GOATA Fluidity	Pg 81
7	Drills And Exercises For GOATA Explosivity	Pg 87
8	Advice For Athletes	Pg 92

1. HOW THE GOATA SYSTEM WAS BORN

Sports are an essential part of my life and always have been. When I was growing up in Louisiana, the men in my family loved watching NBA or NFL games on TV, we were rarely indoors and I was at my happiest when I had a basketball or football in my hands. Over the years, I've become a passionate cyclist and swimmer, and I can hold my own against my brothers on the golf course where they often play with a single-digit handicap. Movement is our thing, and as middle-aged men we are still serious athletes.

But over the years my passion for competition hasn't always served me well. As a kid, most of my coaches were too busy working with other more naturally talented young athletes to make sure that the rest of us were staying strong and balanced as our bodies grew. When I walked or ran, I spread my feet to avoid the chafing pain of my thighs rubbing together and over time, I developed duck feet. My posture was flawed and loads of physical activity during puberty made me an easy mark for Osgood-Schlatter, a condition that causes a hard bunion-like bump to grow just below the kneecap. I can still remember being cut from the varsity basketball team at age sixteen and hearing the coach's explanation which reflected the common attitudes of the time about whether real athletes were made or born. "You got bad feet, and bad hips," my coach barked, "We can't work with you!"

I still held a great passion for playing sports of course—and stayed involved in recreational ball and intramurals. However, without the necessary guidance and attention I soon developed habits that I would later regret in my early and middle adulthood. In high school and college my approach to movement left me exposed to injuries that would keep me off the court or playing field for months at a time. I was still in school when I had my first major back episode, while doing back squats with warm-up weights in the gym. I sought out the help of the family doctor who diagnosed simple back strain and said that the discomfort would go away. After a while I started feeling better, but about ten months later I suffered yet another episode and decided on seeing a specialist. Over the next six years I ended up visiting no less than eight chiropractors, but the acute pain kept returning again and again.

These Doctors were not ignorant, they knew exactly what they were doing—but like many physicians they tended to look at the most immediate source of pain while allowing the underlying causes to go unaddressed, so that relief came in short and fleeting bursts. I had experienced similar problems when I went to see an expert in sports medicine who had me doing simple load-bearing movements on a Nautilus machine to build skeletal muscle. The exercises did little to decompress my spine, even as I made progress with the amount of weight I could move, I didn't feel like I was really getting stronger on a structural level. Things finally came to a head in 1999 before my twenty-ninth birthday when I suffered yet another back episode—my fortieth of all time—after the simple act of sneezing. At this point I needed regular epidural shots just to be comfortable enough to walk and move around. Deeply depressed and unable to play and roughhouse with my three-year-old son, I found a surgeon who proposed an operation to fuse three degenerated discs in my lumbar vertebrae together with a hunk of titanium. Spine surgery is an inherently risky undertaking, and I was anxious about how it would affect my long-term quality of life. I knew that even if the operation was a success my mobility would never be the same again, but at least in theory, I wouldn't be in constant pain.

Two weeks before the surgery was scheduled to take place, I encountered a book titled *Pain Free: A Revolutionary Method for Stopping Chronic Pain* by Pete Egoscue, recommended by Tony Robbins, one of my favorite motivational speakers. At this point, my back and posture problems were so serious that I found it hard to believe that any amount of coaching or low-impact therapy could dig me out of this awful hole. But after reading Pete's book, I was moved to contact him directly and eventually paid him $200 for a remote consultation from his office in San Diego. After spending about $16,000 in medical insurance co-pays, and out-of-pocket payments to chiropractors for at least $35 per session, this felt like a bargain.

Most of my therapy was done using a fax machine. I would

send scanned pictures of myself standing up against a wall and Pete would draw a simple grid over my shoulders, hips, knees, and ankles. On a healthier individual, the lines of the grid would have met in all right angles, but in my own case it was a mess of crooked markers and sharp diagonals with which my shoulders drooped unevenly, my hips protruded outwards and my ankles and knees were splayed open to the sides. I had been involved in competitive sports for years at this point, and it seemed far-fetched that I could have overlooked these simple concepts of muscular and skeletal alignment as badly as I did. It seemed even crazier that I could train myself back into proper posture and mobility.

On the other hand, I'd worked for years as an assistant to my stepfather, an experienced carpenter, who taught me to pay attention to how structures are built to bear weight against the pull of gravity. I was intrigued by how Pete made use of these same concepts in his work as a physical therapist and under his guidance I agreed to delay my back surgery until every corner on my grid was brought to 90 degrees.

My work with Pete was slow and methodical, but dazzlingly effective, and it allowed me to stay active, have fun, and avoid surgery for good. I eventually attended his online classes and in 2008, I travelled to California and became certified as an Egoscue Institute PAS (Postural Alignment Specialist). In the years since, I've recommended his book to athletes, coaches, and trainers—pretty much anyone who wants to stay comfortable and mobile for the next twenty years or more.

Soon, I was back to my favorite sports again, trying new ones, and playing my first full round of golf in at least three years. My approach to exercise and fitness was completely changed and things got particularly interesting when I got involved in spinning—first as a student, then as a teacher—and began training for triathlons hoping to change my body composition and improve my cardiovascular capacity. My first race wasn't pretty—it took me 23 minutes to swim 600 meters—but I was inspired by other competitors many of whom looked surprisingly strong and spry for their ages. In a duathlon three years later, a 68-year-old man left me in the dust during the running portion, even though I was sure I could beat him at first. Granted, lots of people get into triathlons relatively late in life. If you've spent time in the world of endurance sports, you've probably seen men and women with grey hair passing the finish line in the final hour of a marathon or other long- distance race, usually in an awkward shuffle of cramped legs and arms, and clearly enjoying only a fraction of the flexibility and range of motion that they used to. But this guy was different: instead of a bowed back and a stuttering gait, he had an upright posture and moved in easy, open strides. Instead of holding his arms stiffly close to his chest, his hands moved gently at his sides. Despite what must have been decades of compressive sitting—and miles spent on the road—he ran with the mobile hips and the flexible lower-back of a twenty-something stud. It was as if an invisible rope was tied to his waist, gently pulling him through the course. A little later, I invited him to my office to see if there was anything that I could learn from him about sustainable training. I hoped he could share what he knew with my own fitness clients, and one of the first things I asked was if he'd ever been injured. His answer made me laugh out loud. "Well, let's see," he said hesitating, "I strained my hamstring once. That would have been about twenty years ago." At this point, I'd hit a plateau in my development as an athlete and I was ready to look for wisdom elsewhere in the sports medicine and physical therapy worlds. The things I'd learned from Egoscue had been worth way more than the value spent, and I was eternally grateful for the way it allowed me to enjoy the outdoors and avoid surgery—despite my three degenerated discs. But if I was going to continue doing triathlons into my late sixties, I was convinced that there was more I needed to learn. I soon came across the work of Kelly Starrett, a former member of the U.S. national canoe and kayak teams who took up CrossFit in the early 2000s and consolidated his knowledge of human kinetics and sustainable exercise into an enormously popular website called MobilityWOD, and a New York Times bestseller, *Becoming a Supple Leopard*.

A few other authors also had a profound effect on me, including Aaron Mattes (*Active Isolated Stretching*), Kathleen Porter (*Natural Posture for Pain-Free Living*), Esther Gokhale (*8 Steps to a Pain-Free Back*), and Eric Goodman and Peter Park (*Foundation: Redefine Your Core, Conquer*

Back Pain, and Move with Confidence). The knowledge I gained from these "suppleness gurus" was helpful but around the same time that I bought their books I made another purchase that was just as significant in both my own life and in my work as a physical trainer. My first iPad, which proved that neither aspect of my life would ever be the same.

Once I'd figured out how to record clients as they moved around in my studio—and watch the tape in slow-motion, again and again, on apps like Hudl, V1 Golf, and Coach's Eye—I felt newly empowered to find the essential habits of master athletes and to pin down the mistakes that led to athletic overuse, injury and premature fatigue. It became harder to watch sports on TV without wanting to see football or basketball players in slow-motion. But besides professionals, I felt an almost constant urge to look more closely at ordinary people—really anyone who seemed to move without discomfort or pain.

Children were particularly inspiring to me, as were the indigenous people that I watched in documentaries on *National Geographic*. These were classes of people who'd never been to a gym. They'd never been taught "military posture," and yet they seemed to bear weight without wasting energy and could walk and run with remarkable grace. I began to wonder if there was something about the way the rest of us moved that made things more difficult.

Besides using the tablet in my work, pretty soon I was also bugging my friends on social media, watching and eagerly pointing out their mistakes in posture and alignment. There's a chance I got on a few people's nerves but like most posture converts, I'd become a fanatic and couldn't resist sharing my new insights with whomever I thought could benefit. In 2015 I started watching videos produced by David Weck, another slow-motion junkie who had applied his philosophy of posture and movement to develop a line of fitness tools and instructional videos with competitive athletes in mind. By placing an emphasis on coiling core strength, balance and efficiency I was able to take GOATA (Greatest of All Time Athlete or Action) to the next level. Like me, Weck seemed to understand that a game is rarely won in two dimensions; and yet, a stunningly large section of the strength and conditioning community has continued to advocate training in simple exercises based on straight lines and right angles, which all but ignore the way people actually locomote through space.

Powered By GOATA: Move Like the Greatest Of All Time Athletes

Bench presses, military presses, deadlifts and squats can do a lot to build a bodybuilder's physique, but also make it extremely easy to get injured—I wish I had a dime for every person I've met who hurt their knees while doing squats or ruined their shoulders by pushing a massive weight over their heads. More importantly these exercises are incomplete as a preparation for sports, which almost always involve rotation and explosive movement along multiple vectors at once.

In late 2015 I met Gary Scheffler, and we began exchanging ideas about how athletes could overcome bad habits and enhance their natural abilities to become faster, stronger and more agile. I'd been working to devise a set of simple principles for building strength and fluidity to create "GOATAs" and had begun teaching these principles to anyone who wanted to learn. Gary put the icing on the cake and we eventually incorporated the principles of the types of movements needed, in order to create "Explosive GOATAs." Over the past three years we learned to identify the most common posture and alignment problems that lead to injury, and to instruct our clients in movement drills to help them reach their fullest potential—whether they were ordinary enthusiasts—or just trying to be more like elite athletes with professional ambitions.

After watching hundreds of men and women transform their bodies and live healthier pain-free lives, I decided it was time to share this philosophy with an even wider audience. I wrote this book because I think everyone can benefit from hearing the GOATA gospel.

The GOATA 22.5 Degree Set is Developed in the Crawling Phase

The superhuman endurance durable behavior secret is in how we developed, which is the same around the world. It's the late crawling baby with some help from genetics and a family that provides the athlete a movement rich environment, who becomes the super athlete, unless you train the GOATA way of course.

The movement keeps your joints and connective tissue safe for life.

Stand Up Crawling Indicators

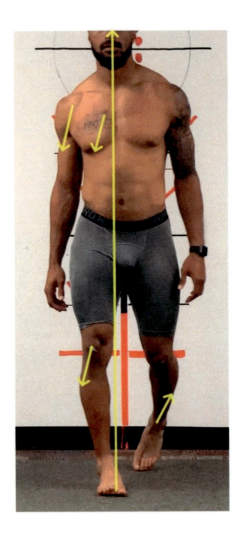

Joseph Este, the first super trained GOATA athlete and master explosive coach

Powered By GOATA: Move Like the Greatest Of All Time Athletes

A GOATA Coach Needs Movement Tools

Use math, simple carpentry tools, and slow motion video to decode or recode super athletes' movements.

2. Pre-Movement Fundamentals

Back Chain vs. Front Chain Dominance

My oldest client is 76 years old, while he isn't the only person past retirement to come to my studio, I've probably helped just as many people in their twenties or teens—especially high school or college athletes who are just starting out and who want to make the most of their inborn talents. It's quite an age range and by being exposed to it every week, I've come to recognize the most common forms of disorganized movement. My job, as I see it, is to help people build the right habits and along the way many clients have also had to unlearn what they were taught by their own teachers and coaches.

What's surprising is that many of the habits that go into efficient locomotion tend to come pretty naturally. If you watch a baby or a young child standing up for the first time, you'll notice that their posture tends to be *back-chain dominant*. They lean on the balls of their feet, with their knees underneath the hips, hips underneath the shoulders, and their shoulders and pelvis drawn back. Whether they're standing or sitting, their spines keep a perfect S-shape: with the rear end sticking slightly outwards, and the hamstrings, glutes, and lats all fully activated. None of this changes when they adopt a "half-squat"—leaning slightly forward, with the chest up, upper back tight, and the rear end dropping just below the knees, everything is unpacked, pliable, and poised for forward motion. But over time, our environment sets us up to move backwards. From sitting at a desk, reclining in an easy chair, sleeping on our bellies, or hunching forward in our chairs to read, type, or text, we eventually adopt a *front-chain dominant* posture. While standing the neck and shoulders are drawn stiffly inwards and the center of the back flexes backwards so that the pelvis moves in front of the gravity line and the head dumps forward unsupported by the rest of the spine. All of this eventually results in the bowed-vertebrae look of a caveman and a Frankenstein-style of walking. The pelvis leads, the spine sits in a static midline over the body, and the rest of the body struggles awkwardly to catch up. Without an expressive curve and coil in our walking pattern, the hips function less like ball-and-socket joints and more like canes or walking sticks which brace us and slow our momentum.

Even if you've never ran a marathon, a front-chain dominant posture can lead to repetitive stress injuries. Flat-footed strength training like flat-footed endurance workouts on an elliptical machine or stationary bike—can result in tiny, acute tears in the Achilles heel or anterior cruciate ligament (ACL). Without a clear pivot point on the outer toes (usually around the fourth or fifth metatarsal), carrying weight on the inside arch causes our feet to pronate and our knees to buckle. This takes the fluidity out of our hips which degrade under the unnatural weight and pressure, while in our midsection the thoracic capsule rounds out wreaking havoc on the lower back. This is further exacerbated when we're sitting still or reclining on our bellies—especially if we sleep on a curved or slightly worn-out mattress.

If there's one thing I've learned over and over as a trainer and coach, it's that the body will adapt to whatever stimulus it's given. Even professional and Olympic athletes with "perfect" genetics can only hope to stay healthy and injury-free by living a Front-chain dominant lifestyle. Luckily, grasping this isn't reserved for the most brilliant doctors or experts in biomechanics. On the contrary, I've always preferred to use clean, simple language when explaining the evolutionary movement coding process involved in helping ordinary people move like great athletes. It can be as simple as telling my clients to emphasize fluidity, force, and explosivity in the muscle groups that are already dominant and maintaining a posture that keeps the back chain of their bodies long and strong.

When Gary and I started working together, we named our system in honor of the Greatest of All Time Athletes because we were convinced that no matter what the sport was, success came to those people who followed the same basic patterns of movement. Once you've broken these patterns down, they seem to appear again and again, whether you are watching Deion Sanders or Serena Williams, Ed Reed, Mirinda Carfrae, Michael

Jordan, or Usain Bolt, they all move the exact same way. Moreover, we knew that if our clients adopted these patterns in their own lives—even if they weren't competitive athletes—then they too, would learn endurance durability and explosive fluidity, and they too, would enjoy a lifetime of pain-free movement. Instead of the two-dimensional pack-and-release style of most weight room training regimens, clients would achieve practical fitness for the real world taking a load-and-explode approach that makes the body flexible, efficient, and durable. Instead of joints and ligaments that ached from being twisted and torqued, all the soreness would be in the muscles which would heal and refortify during post-training recovery. And crucially, that the recovery would be of the highest possible quality: as we all know athletes who perform well on a bench press or force platform are still uncoachable if the pain in their knees, shoulders, or back makes it impossible for them to sleep at night.

Identifying WOATA Habits

When clients first arrive in my office, one of the first things I do is look at how they move by using my own experience as well as the principles I have learned from Pete Egoscue during his Postural Alignment Specialist training. With the help of an iPad, I watch as they do simple squats, hinge their bodies from the waist, stand on one leg, and walk from one end of the room to the other. By taking some photographs or slow-motion video and drawing a grid, I can begin to measure the athlete's landscape and then make up my mind about where their individual weaknesses are. From there we can begin to discuss what the next steps will be in improving their movement game. Some of those weaknesses are easier to spot than others.

A front-chain dominant client will often look goofy or stodgy, or complain about repetitive stress symptoms, rather than trauma from contact or collision sports. During interval training, they might develop Achilles tendonitis, while if they compete in endurance sports, they might be susceptible to hip bursitis, plantar fasciitis, or IT band syndrome. Duck feet, buckling knees, and asymmetries in the shoulders and hips are common, but it's also possible to be front-chain dominant and still look like a model especially if you've done lots of squats, butterfly presses, or bicep curls—imagine someone who looks great at the beach but is too stiff and uncoordinated to enjoy a game of volleyball. These imbalances in the grid are even more prominent once I've tested the client's patterns of locomotion.

Squat

During a squat, **WOATAs** (Worst of All Time Athletes) with uneven posture might have trouble keeping their balance or struggle to shift their body weight along the ridges of their feet and fall on their backs. If the lower back or hamstrings aren't flexible, a client's heels will usually come up off the floor. This is an obvious indicator of front chain dominance, but the biggest sign of trouble is a low inside ankle bone, which limits the natural movement of the knees and can tire out the hips. As a result, a WOATA might have trouble staying in position for more than a few seconds, while a GOATA can hold this pose indefinitely.

Hinge

You don't have to be able to bend your body like a flip-phone to enjoy physical activity but asking a client to touch their toes while standing is a decent way to measure flexibility. During a hinge, a WOATA's back will often be stiff and arched and I can check to see if their hips hover far in front of their knees. This imbalance limits the femurs' ability to rotate in the hip socket so that during the hinge the kneecaps will slide sideways even if the legs are kept perfectly locked. Again, this is a pose that WOATAs will only be able to hold for so long; whereas a seated forward bend will be much easier if you activate the hips and lower abs. A standing hinge is only going to be comfortable if you're back-chain dominant and your hamstrings and glutes are open and loose.

Stork Stand

If you're front-chain dominant then it will be difficult to stand on one leg without either leaning unnaturally far back or allowing your body weight to move to the inside edge of your planted foot. When this happens the ankle bone collapses downward, the knee shifts out to the side and it becomes almost impossible to hold the hips so that they're parallel to the floor. Most of the time instead of the shoulders sitting directly above the hips, one hip will jut outwards and one shoulder will either hike up or droop down below the other.

Walking

If you've ever tried running without moving your arms, you know that shifting weight from side to side is particularly important for maintaining balance and momentum during endurance training. If we can't harness that momentum properly then our hips and knees will often function like a set of brakes, opening us up to overuse and fatigue.

Granted, low inside ankle bones and outwardly splayed kneecaps may not do a lot of harm when we're standing still. But in movement, WOATAs invariably spend extra energy by pushing themselves sideways with one foot and then stabilizing the body with the other. The potential for waste is enormous as is the exposure to injury and this only gets worse when the athlete accelerates. Without a symmetrical, forward-facing stride, front-chain dominant athletes tend to push themselves from one end of the room to the other with the weakest least stable part of their calves and quadriceps. Over longer or more strenuous runs, they will continue to strike the ground on the insides of their feet putting unnecessary torque on their knees and adding extra weight to the load on their hips and lower back.

Identifying GOATA Habits

Newton's second law of motion defines force as the product of mass and acceleration. As an athlete and trainer, I've come to believe that how we handle that force will determine how comfortably we move through space. Through centuries of evolution the body has been conditioned to absorb and redirect force and weight through the natural bends and curved edges in our bones and joints and we overlook these bends and curves at our own risk. On the other hand, those of us who take full advantage of the built-in engines of the human skeleton—and its natural ability to cycle, whip, and swing, can learn to make the most of our genetic potential and become stronger, faster, and more durable than we ever thought possible.

Squat

In almost any position back-chain dominant athletes will have high inside ankle bones, forward-facing toes, and knees that flex away from the navel as well as strong hamstrings and a supple lower back. Their spines keep the same marvelous S-shape whether they're standing up straight or crouching into a paleo squat and when they approach the floor there's no need to hold out their arms to keep balance. Without tightening the core and even if they haven't done loads of exercises on their abs or hip abductors, GOATAs can rest almost all their weight on their heels with their rear ends nearly touching the floor.

Hinge

Protecting the lumbar curve is essential to staying mobile and pain-free as we age and athletes who keep their backs flexible and strong will garner considerable rewards on the playing field. I've got nothing against rope climbs and pull- ups but there's not much use in developing traps and lats if you're too muscle-bound to swim or throw a ball. This is why the standing hinge is such an effective diagnostic tool: not all GOATAs can touch the floor with their palms while their knees are locked but most of them can and beyond measuring the strength of their lower core and the looseness of their arms and hamstrings, I've found that athletes who master this position can learn to gain momentum and power by gently whipping their shoulders from side to side as they move.

Stork Stand

Asymmetrical poses make it all the easier to appreciate the

cyclical overlapping engines that make up GOATA movement. In a one-legged stork stand, back-chain dominant athletes will still have their feet and knees facing straight forward with the knee of the planted leg directly above the ankle, the hip directly above the knee, and the shoulder directly above the hip. It's easy for them to hold the position, with their weight evenly distributed on the planted foot but they are always poised for the next step; more advanced athletes might allow the head to hover over the raised leg so that the shoulders and torso are ready to whip back and forth with the hips.

Walking

All of this comes together once a GOATA is moving forward. During the first stride, the head and torso hover directly over the landing foot which once again, faces directly forward with the inside ankle bone high. Once this foot hits the ground the ankle—instead of moving along one dimension—*corners*, moving weight from the heel to the fourth or fifth metatarsal before finally pushing off from the ball of the foot. You can also see the cornering effect at the knee (which flexes *away* from the navel) and in the opposite hip which turns *towards* the navel. Upstairs, the shoulder above the planted foot mirrors the movement of the knee moving *towards* the navel until the opposite heel lands on the ground. This twisting and coiling is meant to be subtle—always there, but never exaggerated and the only time the knees or chest should be facing directly forward is at the exact midpoint of each stride at the moment the knee on the planted leg is just about locked.

Running

Believe it or not, almost nothing changes once a GOATA starts to pick up speed. As one-foot pivots off of the fourth or fifth metatarsal the opposite foot launches forward and the heel touches down bearing the weight with the midfoot. By this point, the three main engines of the body—hips, shoulders, and spine—start to go to work in synchronicity. The shoulder rotates down and about 22.5 degrees backwards which the upper arm mirrors by pumping 22.5 degrees inwards. Along the trunk of the body, the spine rotates 22.5 degrees back bending slightly towards the

Powered By GOATA: Move Like the Greatest Of All Time Athletes

extended leg. All of this is guided by the movement of the head which hovers directly over the feet as they hit the ground. After they push off, the heel points up and outwards, away from the body.

Getting these three engines to work in concert will convert a daily training run from a painful grind of hips and knees into an expression of pure joy. But you don't have to be an endurance athlete to put these principles to work. Part of the reason why I've been able to help such a wide range of athletes—from football players to baseball players and golfers to martial artists—is because the key movements of almost every major sport can be broken down into the same three phases that make up a runner's stride. Inspired by the greatest coaches of all time from the swim and golf community worlds like Jack Nicklaus's mentor, the late Jack Grout, I teach in phases, particularly three distinct phases. In swimming, the hand grabs water, pulls and releases the water and then recovers the arm; and in golf it's the back swing, downswing, and follow through. I refer to these in GOATA as *drop in and load, corner and explode* and *release and reset*.

For martial artists, a well-developed roundhouse kick is a great example. During the *drop-in* phase a fighter in an orthodox stance will step the left leg forward and lead with the right shoulder. This puts torque into the other two engines of the body loading the hips and spine like a spring. A front-chain dominant athlete as experts might notice, will instead lead with their hips which makes extra work for the hip abductors and can-do damage to the joint over time in addition to cutting into the momentum of the kicking foot. A back-chain dominant fighter, by contrast, will feel like they're about to crack a whip: during the *cornering* phase, the left hip moves 22.5 degrees away from the navel while on the right side, the spine and trunk shift 22.5 degrees forward. All of this happens before the foot has ever left the ground, when the foot leaves the ground it smashes into the target with maximum fluidity and power. Finally, the fighter rotates right back into position during the *reset* period with no loss of balance so that it's easy to move into another combination or block an opponent's strikes.

You can also see these three phases when a pitcher throws a baseball. Anyone with a background in the game has encountered the cliché of a talented player whose shoulder finesse has started to wane—the locker room is overrun with spent hot packs, empty bottles of ibuprofen and melted bags of ice, while tougher cases become candidates for surgery— but it doesn't have to be this way. In my experience the real secret to preserving a "golden arm" is to stop relying on it and to instead focus on the core engines that help create a perfect fastball. This means staying loose during the *drop-in* phase, focusing on the hips and quads as you wind-up and allowing the spine and torso to drift gently back and away from the batter. The shoulder should be the last engine to cycle back so that during the *cornering* phase, the arm—just like a kickboxer's shin—will feel like the end of a cracking whip. Also just like a kickboxer, the *reset* phase will feel steady and smooth and the pitcher will have no trouble getting right back into position after releasing the ball and following through.

Perhaps the most compelling example of a GOATA's three phases of movement is a golfer's swing. Cutting down the thousand-and-one details that instructors say are essential to a perfect drive, I tell my clients to pay attention to the same three engines. During *drop in*, a master golfer chooses the right pivot points and sticks with them keeping the knees bent and the feet comfortably planted as the body weight shifts and the waist twists gently away from the navel. The spine and hips lead the way and the shoulders, arms, and hands stay fairly stiff until the very peak of the backswing so that the wrists only break when they're about the same height as the ears. The order of operations is the same in the *cornering* phase of the downswing during which a GOATA will take full advantage of the natural curves in the spine, hip sockets, knees, and ankles all while keeping the muscles above the waist steady and loose. To put it another way: Even if you want the ball to move straight along just two dimensions, you'll need your body to operate along three dimensions to maximize distance and accuracy. This is also seen during *release and reset*: the shaft of the club doesn't have to be parallel to the ground when you're following through nor does the grip ever have to be directly above your head. You'll know you did it right because the entire swing will feel slow, unified, and symmetrical—and because the ball will go exactly where you want it to.

Even normal folks can appreciate the beauty of a harmonious spine, hip, and shoulder engine by watching my favorite model of GOATA movement: a baby's crawl. It sounds crazy but in my opinion, eight-month-olds making their way across a living room rug often show more efficiency and coordination than most adult marathoners do during the first mile of a race. No one has to tell them to activate their core or keep their heads up and yet small children will somehow manage to maintain a smooth curve in their backs and gently rotate their hips and spine 22.5 degrees in each direction as each leg moves forward. Just like elite sprinters, they will move their arms and shoulders in such a way as to complement and mirror the movement of the torso so that the elbow runs 22.5 degrees back around the body at the same time that the leg is pulled up towards the chest. Lastly, after *cornering* and *releasing*, you'll notice that their heels are pointed up and outwards with which they seem to know how to do before they've even learned how to walk.

I sometimes wonder if trainers like me would be out of business if more adults paid attention to the natural athleticism of their children. However, until that day comes, I'll be showing my clients how to be back chain dominant by having them move across the floor on their hands and knees starting from the referee's position of a collegiate wrestler. I spend a lot of time on the floor myself, even when I'm not at work just as a way of keeping my posture centered and my hips and lower-back supple and loose. If you've lost track of what proper alignment really feels like then there's no better way to restore it than by looking back at what you did when you were first learning to move.

Back Chain Dominant Musculature Looks like a slight pike where the haunches are behind the ribcage and the spine is long and decompressed.

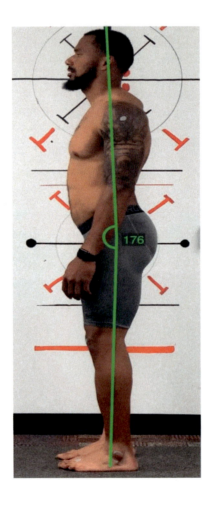

Back-chain dominant (BCD) means haunches keeps the spine long, decompressed, and safe

Front and Back Chain Comparison

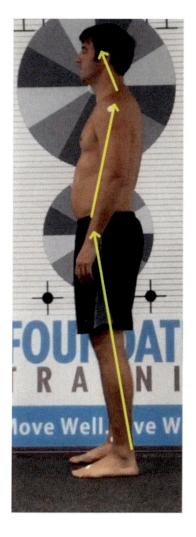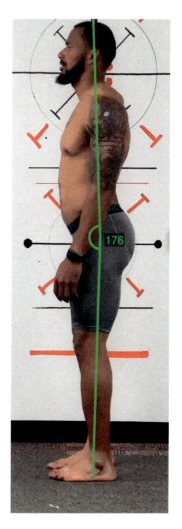

Front-chain dominant versus back-chain dominant

Jose G Boesch

The GOATA, Diego Maradona and a toddler from the book " Ageless Spine" by Kathleen Porter

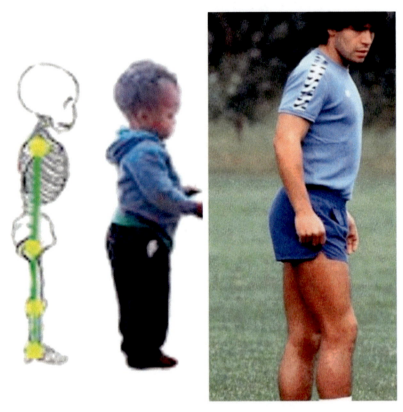

The super athlete's back-chain dominant shape is the same as the toddlers

Back Chain Movement

Haunches are below or behind a decompressed spine and ribcage

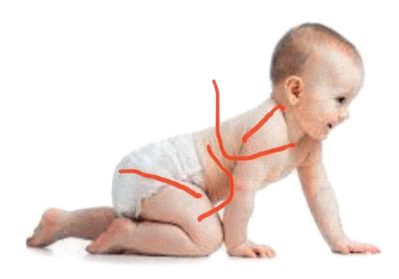

The development of movement coding of all humans will guide the way to the super mover

GOATA Crawling Indicators
The 22.5 degree Set

Master GOATA Coach Joseph Este shows the crawling pattern which equates to his sub 4.3 40-yard dash run times

GOATA Running Indicators

The 22.5 degree Set

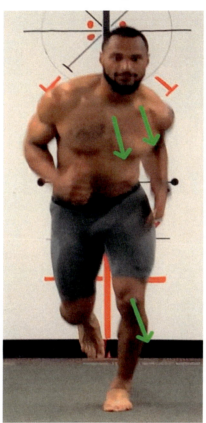

GOATA stand-up crawling is super forward locomotion

Back Chain Dominant Toddlers

The GOATA Toddlers Alyx and Gary Scheffler Jr. using flawless BCD strength and balance

BCD GOATA Squat

GOATA Joseph Este's flawless BCD squat pose

BCD GOATA Hinge

GOATA Joseph Este's flawless BCD hinge pose

Powered By GOATA: Move Like the Greatest Of All Time Athletes

Stand up crawling indicators

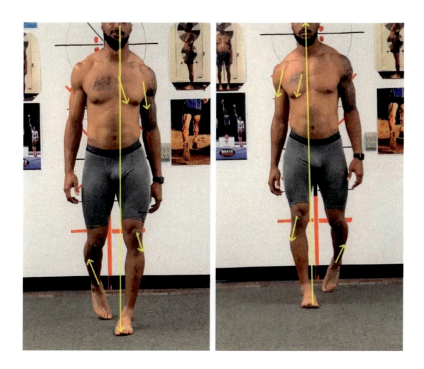

Comparison

The stand-up crawling, walking and running indicators are identical to a creeping or crawling baby in super athletes

BCD GOATA Stork

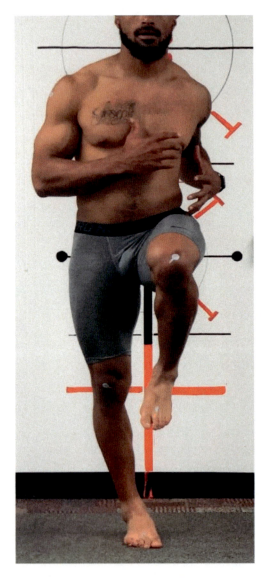

The GOATA stork phase in Phase 2 gives clues to elite movers

WOATA Irregular or Imbalanced Shape

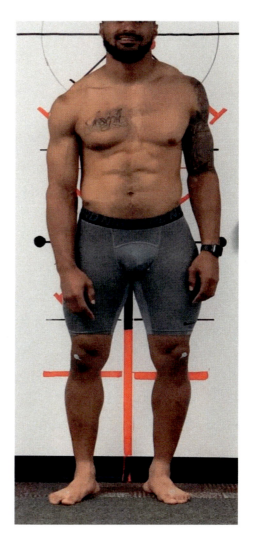

WOATA pre-cornered packed trunk

WOATA Irregular or Imbalanced Hinge

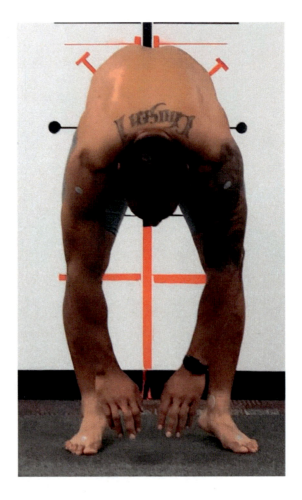

WOATA imbalances are numerous from feet pointed out to a tight back chain

WOATA Front Chain Dominant musculature rib cage or behind haunches

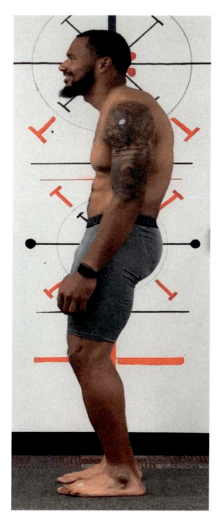

WOATA head and knees moving in the front-chain

WOATA Irregular or Imbalanced Squat

WOATA feet pointing out

WOATA Irregular or Imabalanced Stork

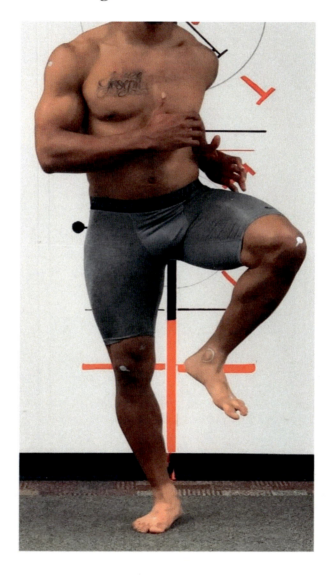

WOATA feet, hip, and spine all misbehaving

WOATA Walking

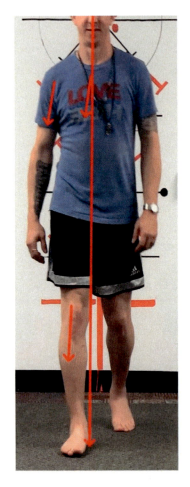 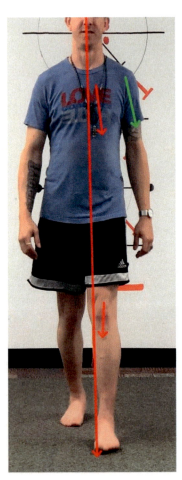

WOATA spine is too stiff and hips moving in reverse, inside ankle bones low and more

3. Training to Perfect GOATA Movement

Basic Shape Exercises

As their initial assessment and scoring, I generally ask new clients to start on a few movements to help them get a better grasp of effective cornering and to improve their skeletal alignment.

Head and Neck

The first part of the routine involves extending the rear end back by two or three inches, clasping the hands behind the lower back, and steadily circling the head around the shoulders like a gyroscope, five times in each direction. This is followed by five exaggerated nods, slowly lifting the chin all the way up, then lowering it all the way back down. If the neck is drooping too far forward this exercise corrects the position of the head so that it hovers more comfortably above the shoulders.

Upper Back

To reverse the caved-in chest of a front-chain dominant athlete, I'll have clients extend the arms straight out at their sides, extend the rear end by two or three inches, pinch the shoulder blades together, and draw the shoulders back in. From here, you can learn to corner with the shoulders by making small circles with the hands, forward with the palms down, and then backward with the palms up. I usually follow this with some elbow curls which involve touching the temple of the head with each hand and moving the elbows from the sides to the center of the chest, while the upper arms stay parallel to the floor.

Thoracic Capsule

Now we're ready to move on to another gyroscope, located just below the sternum. To get used to the sensation I call *pack-and-release*, I have clients draw the shoulders down and inward with the head lowered, then pinch the shoulder blades back together while lifting the head back up. After two or three repetitions, we add a twist, continuing the pack-and-release movement, while simultaneously rotating the upper torso, clockwise around the hips. After five or six circles, we change direction and do five or six counterclockwise rotations. This too, is meant as a cornering exercise for the spine, and so a key thing to remember is to have the chest muscles fully engaged when bending forward, and to have the shoulder blades fully pinched-in when bending back.

Hips

At this point, each foot should be placed directly beneath the hip socket and the toes should be pointed inwards, to exaggerate the 22.5-degree inward bend of a GOATA's running stride. By slowly hinging up and down at the waist for three or four reps, a client will learn to recognize the sensation of cornering in the hip socket. To enhance that sensation even more, we complicate the gentle up-and-down bending at the waist with a hula-hoop twist so as to mirror the movement we did with the shoulders and back. All of this does a great deal to correct the posture mistakes that lead to back pain; by loosening up the upper vertebrae; cornering exercises like these tend to correct the hunched-over stance of front-chain dominant athletes teaching them to adopt a more neutral resting place for their head and neck when leaning back.

Ankles

Standing on one leg, I'll have clients lace their fingers under their raised thigh and make a few circles in each direction with the foot. This is followed by yet another pack-and-release, in which the client's toe curls up towards the shin (the "pack") and then extends straight out (the "release"). We repeat the process with the other ankle.

After this, it's time to start loading the column. This begins with the use of a slant-board—a simple wedge-shaped tool whose top surface is angled 22.5 degrees up from the surface of the floor—which I have clients stand on with their backs against the wall for 30 seconds to a minute at a time usually for a total of ten minutes. The toes point upward and obviously, this helps to stretch the calves and hamstrings but what's really important is to make clients more used to the feeling of having everything lined-up and symmetrical with the feet about a hip-width apart and the knees pointing straight forward. The legs keep their orientation when I take the slant-board away and I have clients lean their backs against the wall and pretend there's an invisible chair under their rear end. In most workouts this wall-sit can last up to four minutes.

By this point, even a first-time client will begin to understand how it feels to stand up with back-chain dominant posture. But if they're still leading with the hips and the shoulders behind the rear end or their head is drooping forward—then there's still more work we can do.

Half-Squat

A great exercise to move onto is a little like the *utkatasana* (chair pose) that's taught in some yoga studios. The knees are about hip width apart, the feet are parallel, the rear end sticks out, and the chin points up and forward. I'll have my clients hold this position while they do a gentle hinge at the waist, while the chest moves upwards towards the ceiling, then lowers towards the floor. After about twelve minutes we can try out a contralateral locomotive version of the same movement: we still hinge at the waist but this time one-foot steps back and carries the weight on the fourth or fifth metatarsal instead of the heel. This is a quintessentially three-dimensional exercise and is especially helpful for improving running form since most clients will instinctively load their haunches on the side of the planted leg and rotate the shoulder downwards and back while the knee on the other leg bends 22.5 degrees toward the navel—exactly what they should do. After a few up-and-down bends, we switch legs, and do the same load-and-corner movement on the other side.

Squinge

What comes next is a combination of a hinge and a squat, starting with the feet a little further than shoulder-width apart. From this position it's often a good idea to try the same basic shape movements I have clients do during the start of the workout: extending the hands out to their sides, making small circles with the arms, moving the hands up and down in front of them, or rotating at the waist. Another great exercise involves touching the floor, shifting weight from side to side, and cornering through either hip socket, then slowly straightening the legs, until you're more or less upright. By this point the hamstrings, glutes, and lower back should feel blown up and fully activated—a sure sign that the client is learning to be back-chain dominant.

Later, we'll begin to focus more on suppleness. Baseball players for example might try more traditional upper body stretches, by placing a hand on the wall and twisting the torso in the opposite direction opening up the chest and bicep. Football players might benefit from getting into a lunge and leaning forward for a few seconds, then leaning back, to loosen and improve circulation in the hip.

Building Locomotive Systems

At the next stage, I'll arrange two slant-boards face to face to create a sloped surface with both sides running 22.5 degrees upwards towards the center. If clients aren't already used to keeping a high inside ankle bone during their squats or hinges, the added equipment makes this easier to learn. They start with a squat, sticking out the rear end, and slowly moving it back, while leaning slightly forward. Once they feel the stretch in their hamstrings, clients should slowly bend their legs while keeping the chest and chin high until the knees are below the hips. From here, they extend the rear end up towards the ceiling, pulling the torso into a half-squat, and then allowing the legs to straighten, so that the chest and shoulders continue to rise until they're standing straight up.

Powered By GOATA: Move Like the Greatest Of All Time Athletes

A hinge is just a little trickier: the rear end instead of moving out and down, moves out and up. Again, once clients feel the stretch in their hamstrings they can reach downwards to the floor, or to the peak in the middle of the two slanted boards.

If I'm convinced a client is truly owning the high-inside ankle bone in these exercises I make things more interesting by adding in some pivot-point calf raises. At the low-point of the squat or the hinge, the goal should be to carry the body weight at the fourth and fifth metatarsals and then lift the heels up off of the slant-boards so that clients can feel the exact point where they should be pushing off. From there, the goal would be to combine everything into a smooth, unified movement: starting with the squat, reaching the hands downward for a hinge, returning to the squat, straightening the legs and back, and cornering at the pivot-points on the feet.

Contralateral Movement

Pretty soon, most clients will be hankering for something a little more rooted in the real world. The slant-boards stay in the mix, but instead of having them face-to-face, I'll move one board about a stride-length in front of the other to mimic a master runner's form. During the *drop-in*, the chest rotates out towards the front knee, which itself moves 22.5 degrees outwards as it bends. If you could draw a line that begins at the front toe and extends behind the front heel, the head should be directly above it and the upper arm should rotate 22.5 degrees backwards towards the spine. The next step is to rise back up, straighten the legs, and practice the same movement on the back foot; again, the chest and knee go out, the foot is pointed straight forward, the head is above the line of the foot, and the upper arm rotates 22.5 degrees back. More often than not, a client who can move comfortably from these two *drop-ins*—shifting back and forth between the front and back leg—will begin to look like an Olympic marathoner.

The second way I teach contralateral *drop-ins* is by using a wall or a column. With one hand posted the opposite leg is bent

22.5 degrees outwards, while the other hip coils inwards, the chest stays high, and the spine stays long and loose. After this, I have clients switch arms and go through the same movement with the other leg, until they look comfortable with it.

The next step is to try *cornering*. After the *drop-in*, the knee rotates back towards the navel, until it faces directly forward and the spine straightens back up. It might sound funny to suggest you can improve your running technique without moving the planted foot but as this exercise illustrates, the best runners in the world tend to pull their bodies *past* and *around* their feet with each step, rather than shifting or dragging their feet across the ground. Faster times after all go to whomever has the longest stride and spends the least amount of time with their feet on the ground and so the perfect runner's form tends to use the sole of the foot as a static object. Another way to see this is to watch world-class rowers or swimmers—like Mark Spitz—both of whom know better than to waste their energy by moving an oar or a hand *through* the water. Instead, the oar or hand behaves like an anchor and more or less stays still while the rest of the body corners *past* and *around* it to move forward.

Cross Over Tracer

The last thing to do with a wall or column is the *release and reset*, which I tend to teach with one leg directly in front of the other and with a very slight bend in either knee. The back-leg *drops in* and *corners* rotating from the heel to the pivot point on the fourth metatarsal, while the front heel scrapes up along the back shin. When the back leg is fully straight, the back heel should point 22.5 degrees out and the front knee should be poised for the next step at just a slightly lower height than it would be during a steady jog or run. We then repeat this sequence with the legs reversed. When I see clients doing this properly, I know they have learned GOATA locomotion in its most fundamental form.

GOATA Neck Gyroscope Rolls Series

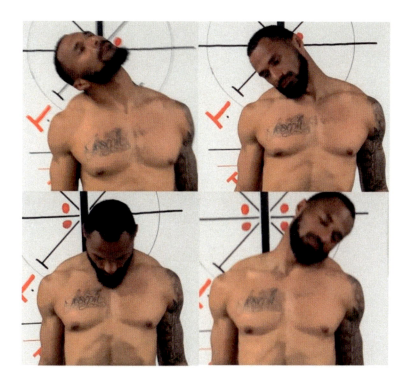

Use the human internal gyroscopes to re-balance and code super movement. 1. Neck gyroscope

Shoulder Gyro Series

2a. Shoulder gyroscope: Pack, corner, and release arm circles

Elbow Curls – Part of Shoulder Gyro Series

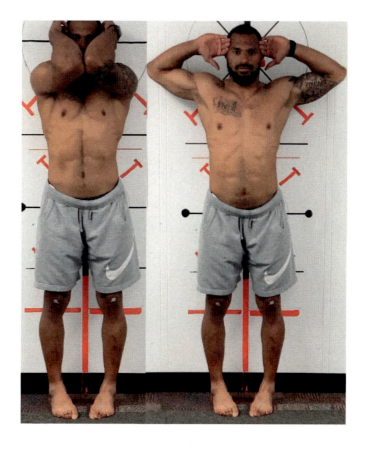

2b. Shoulder gyroscope: Pack and release elbow curls

Mid Back Gyro Series

3. Rib-cage gyroscope: Pack, corner, and release circle waves

Hip Gyro Series Squinge – Push Forward

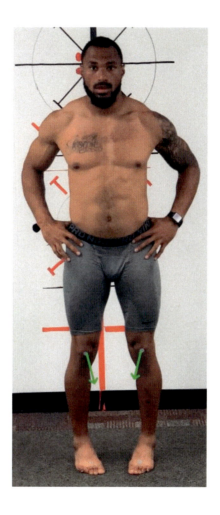

4a. Hip gyroscope: Moving hips in same pack, corner release circle waves

Hip Gyro Series Squinge – Knees In

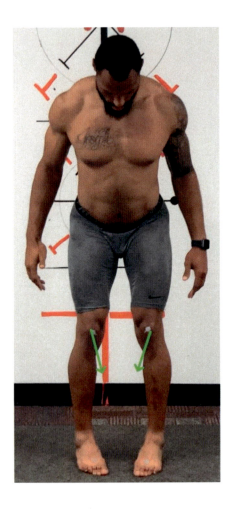

4b. Hip gyroscope: Pack releases similar to yoga cat cow, but at hips

Ankle Gyro Series

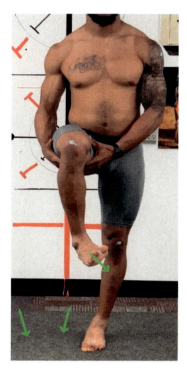 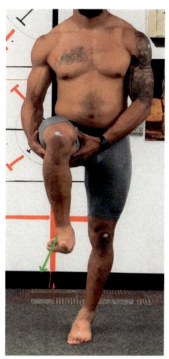

5. Ankle gyroscope: Pack, corner release circle waves and pack release point flexes

Align Series Wall Drop – All Load Joints Aligned with Gravity

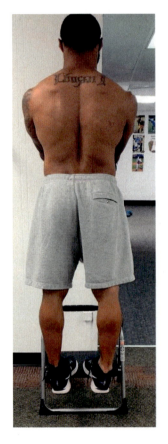

Column reorganizing using a standard small ladder; Ten-minute recommended hold

Level Series Align the Hip, Knee, and Ankle Joints

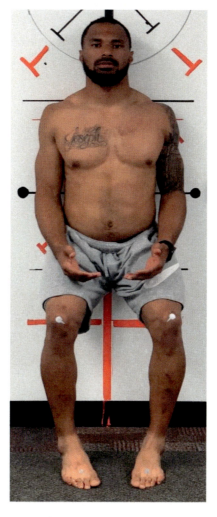

Column reorganizing building the hip, knee, and foot column

4. In the Studio

Joe Este

Joe Este a Louisiana native, didn't take the traditional route to become a professional football player. In fact, he identified mostly as a baseball player growing up and despite being a devoted Saints and LSU fan all his life, he didn't play a game of tackle until around the seventh grade. But during his years at Alfred Bonnabel Magnet Academy High School in Kenner, recruiters were impressed by his work ethic and natural athleticism. After spending two years building his academics at Copiah-Lincoln Community College, he got in touch with the coaching staff at the University of Tennessee at Martin, where he eventually distinguished himself as a tough, tenacious defensive back. In 2018 after tallying 129 tackles and four interceptions during his two seasons with the Skyhawks, Joe signed as an undrafted free agent with the Tennessee Titans. Though he was later waived by the team, the Winnipeg Blue Bombers expressed interest a few months later and he eventually signed a contract.

Joe attended camp with Ed Reed and learned to cover deep passes with precision from watching Deion Sanders, a family friend. But despite having superb instincts—and no shortage of role models—things have not always gone smoothly. He broke his collarbone twice in high school and suffered two torn meniscuses in junior college during a summer practice before his sophomore year. After trying to play through the pain, he visited the team trainer who recommended he see a doctor, and an MRI revealed tears in both the lateral and medial meniscus which would require arthroscopic surgery to treat. Though Joe recovered quickly and was jogging comfortably just a few days after the operation, the pain creeped back and was almost always on his mind during his years at UT Martin.

Through Don Cox—who works as a defensive back specialist for Under Armour and is one of Joe's oldest mentors—I got in touch with Joe and suggested he come to GLS Training Facility

Powered By GOATA: Move Like the Greatest Of All Time Athletes

for a consultation. When he came to my office, I started talking to him about my background and we spent a little time discussing how posture and alignment might be at the root of his knee problems. Joe states, "He told me about the corrective system, which I didn't know much about, it was a strange, foreign language to me." During his first session, I went through my normal battery of diagnostic tests, having Joe stand, walk, squat, and hinge, with small green stickers on his ankles and knees so that I could watch how they shifted as he moved. After taking some still photographs and looking at slow-motion video, I could see where he had run into trouble. Though he was naturally bow-legged, Joe was duck footed when he ran and his hips and knees didn't rotate properly when he picked up speed. A lot of his front-chain dominance seemed to come from his habits in high school during which he paid minimal attention to his posture and spent most of his time in the weight room building up his chest and arms.

To begin working on Joe's cornering and to improve how he lined up his femurs when he ran, I started him on a regimen of seated knee squeezes: having him squeeze a pad between his legs for a few seconds at a time, doing sets of 100 reps each. We also incorporated some squats to get his hips open and rotating elevating his toes with a slant-board and using standing knee squeezes with his back against the wall. These were meant to strengthen his hip adductors and were done for three sets of 40. To strengthen his traps and lats we introduced some reverse flies with elastics—pulling a rubber band-type rope apart and over his head, for four sets of twenty—as well as some superman raises—lifting his arms, legs, and chest off the floor for a few seconds at a time.

When we first met, Joe's 40-yard dash was around 4.4 or 4.5. Bringing this down was one of his main goals, and from an early session I could see that he was leaving a lot of talent and speed out on the field. There was room for improvement in the way in which he coiled his spine and instead of using his arms to complement the closing of his hips on each stride, he tended to pump them straight up down which drove his body weight into the ground. After watching some slow-motion video, we spent the first couple of months focusing on exercises that would help him use his spinal, hip, and shoulder engines more efficiently. I coached him on some release drills with a spinning board, which helped to strengthen the outside of calves as well as knee-over-opposite foot cat walks which improved the cornering in his hips. Then I added weighted side bends which opened up his spinal engine even more. Every two weeks we checked his 40-yard dash and after a while, the hard work paid off. During the Winnipeg try-outs Joe blew the recruiting staff away by running a 4.35 during the 40-yard dash.

As of this writing, Joe still has a few more months to prepare for the Bombers training camp, and his goal is to simply sharpen his tools and be even faster than he was last year. A typical day will start with weight training at 4:30 a.m., followed by position drills in the afternoon and a couple of hours in the GLS Training Facility in the evening. His future looks extremely bright, but even if Joe wasn't a professional athlete, I like to think he has benefited from what he has learned from GOATA & GLS about leading a pain-free lifestyle.

"I was tired of hurting, and I want to be the best of the best," he later said. "A lot of what I learned was just common sense, but once you really buy into it and start asking questions, and really pay attention, its life changing. And not just for athletes who go to the gym every day."

Doug Foreman

Given his background in the medical equipment business it felt a little ironic for Doug Foreman to end up in an exam room with some of the same surgical X-rays he sold for a living. It just so happens that despite having an extensive background in health and fitness and leading an active lifestyle since he was a teenager, Doug was suffering from chronic back pain by his mid-thirties. Spending long hours in his car for work probably didn't help either, and on occasion, the discomfort was so severe that even standing up could be difficult.

"A few times, it just locked up," he said. "I couldn't move. I had to get injections just to get up off the couch."

For the next few years, Doug visited every expert in pain management under the sun. Doctors and physical therapists broached the topic of surgery, but what really bothered him was

Powered By GOATA: Move Like the Greatest Of All Time Athletes

their advice that he should avoid the physical activities he'd pursued for fun, including martial arts like kickboxing, tai chi, kung fu, and Krav Maga.

"I really didn't like those answers," he said. "Being told that I couldn't do those things anymore was not going to work."

Things started looking up after Doug started meeting with Mary Beth Vorion, an expert in the active isolated stretching methods developed by Aaron Mattes, whose approach helped him overcome some of the pain and discomfort. Eventually, Mary Beth suggested he visit GLS Training Facility to see if working out with Gary and me could improve his strength and flexibility. Doug finally made an appointment in the winter of 2018. We talked for a little bit about the science and philosophy that informed our work, and I went through my normal routine of watching him squat, hinge, and walk, putting bright green stickers on his knees, ankles, and feet to see how they cornered when he travelled across the room.

Of course, we already knew that the range of motion in Doug's lower body felt pretty tight and restricted. But what he didn't seem to realize—despite his experience looking at fluoroscopic images of human skeletons—was that his own hips and pelvis were underutilized when he walked or ran. From looking at slow motion video for example, I could see that he wasn't pushing the femoral head of either leg back into the hip socket which made him feel stiffer and robbed him of a lot of power. For years, Doug believed he'd had trouble touching his toes because his hamstrings were tight, but the more we looked at his posture, the more we realized that the real culprit was front-chain dominance in his hips.

One of the first things I had him work on were hinges and squats with face-to-face slant-boards which helped him get a better feel of where he needed to be carrying weight and pushing off. As it turned out, a lot of his martial arts training in animal movement had involved an open-footed, front-chain dominant stance, and so it took some time for him to relearn these exercises. Over the next few months, this had a profound effect on Doug's regular training runs, not just because he was engaging his glutes for greater stride length but also from improvements in the way he turned his shoulders and adjusted his center of gravity. From looking at slow-motion video during almost every session—we could watch and see how he began to emphasize an entirely new set of muscles.

As you can probably guess, this translated into enormous changes in how he kicked. Exercises such as the leg raises he did in sets of twenty while leaning against a wall—this helped Doug learn how to corner, shift weight, and land on either foot, all of which are essential to the coil-and-release effect of a strong and dynamic roundhouse kick. Over time, Doug also got better at harnessing energy with his arms and shoulders and releasing that energy as he rotated his hips and core, so that his strikes were smooth, balanced, and confident when they hit their target. Some of the improvement was also probably due to his work with our strength coach using weights and resistance bands along with more traditional power exercises like squats.

"There are foundational elements to the way we move," Doug says. "If those aren't correct, then you're basically reseeding bad patterns, which causes a lot of pain over time. Before doing something drastic, I would first take a real hard look at the foundation of how you're moving and how you're standing and fix it in your own way."

Doug has a home gym, equipped with a heavy bag, a BOSU® half dome, some resistance bands, a squat bar, and a shrug bar, as well as a set of slant-boards which he uses almost every day. The gear has made it easy for him to build on what he's learned from GLS Training Facility on his own, and continue his education in kickboxing, which includes sparring a couple of days a week. Not too long ago he travelled to Thailand and worked out at a few Muay Thai gyms, and he's given some thought to entering a masters-level tournament. Mostly though, his priority is to maintain as much endurance and flexibility as he can so that he can continue to enjoy the sports he participates in without any unnecessary interventions.

"I've gained a completely new way to manage my own body," he says. "I've changed a lot—almost everything about the way that I stand, sit, and drive—and I feel like I have the tools that I need to not be in pain all the time, and to hopefully not have to get surgery. It's given me a way to stay physically active and do the things that I love."

Donald Clay Jr.

A rising college freshman, who found out about GLS from our postings on social media, Donald is one of the younger athletes to come through our doors. Unlike other clients he wasn't overcoming any ailments related to collision, trauma or overuse; rather than seeking us out to address chronic pain or joint problems, his priority was to build good habits while he was still young so as to better harness his natural abilities as a football player and preserve the assets he was born with over the long haul.

Those assets are considerable, playing cornerback for John Curtis Christian School, Donald was ranked among the top fifteen players in the Greater New Orleans area during his senior year, making 39 tackles and breaking up ten passes. Teammates elected him team captain in recognition of his strong work ethic and intelligent approach to the game and he caught the eye of the recruiters. Ultimately, he received no less than twenty offers from programs around the country, including Kentucky and Arizona State, before finally committing to Southern Methodist University, who offered an impressive scholarship. His long-term ambition is to play in the NFL and in order to get there, Donald has put a premium on staying supple and continuing to grow.

"No matter how hard you work or how good you are, if you can't stay injury-free, you can't show your talent," Clay proclaims. "Knock on wood, I haven't been off the field for those kinds of reasons."

Donald wasn't the only recruited athlete in his class at John Curtis, which happens to have one of the most dominant football teams in the region, and the school coaches' approach to strength and conditioning has been consistently healthy and robust, if a bit conventional. In addition to the footwork drills and lateral work he did during practice, weightlifting sessions were devoted to power movements like bench presses, squats, and cleans, in addition to the curls, calf raises, and tricep extensions he did to build smaller muscle groups. Donald was eager to try something a little more experimental and given how early the Training Facility was in its development, the training he did with us was a learning experience for both Gary and me.

During our first session, we talked a little bit about the role of back-chain dominance and how it factored into every form of efficient movement—from the way babies plodded across a living room, to the way Usain Bolt ran on a track. Donald was interested in making his hips stronger, improving his alignment, lateral quickness, and explosivity; so, most of his workouts during the first few weeks focused on those areas. Notwithstanding Donald's experience as a sprinter and hurdler, there were also some things we felt we could teach him about running form, including dropping in and opening up his stride, so we gave some additional attention to his 40-yard dash. Overall, this included doing some infant crawls and cat walks on all fours, as well as a lot of circuit-based training, in which we'd choose five to eight exercises and have him spend two minutes on each station.

One of the most effective stations Donald worked was the weighted sled. Proper cornering is crucial to this exercise and so when he got into position and started pushing, we made a special effort to ensure he was pivoting on the fourth and fifth metatarsal with each step and that he maintained the same width between his feet that he used while running, all while resisting the temptation to fall into a tight-rope style, heel-over-toe form as he moved the sled forward. Squats with a medicine ball were also a useful tool since they helped him to learn a back-chain dominant approach to carrying weight, which he could feel from his heels when he extended his legs and all the way into his upper body when he released the ball. Another squat-based exercise involved the VertiMax platform, during which Donald wore a belt that was attached to elastic bands which were hooked up to the surface he was standing on. As with the other stations, this required paying extra attention to keeping his chest up, knees over toes, and feet parallel, so that he could use the full range of motion in his hips and glutes.

Additional exercises included ladder steps, to improve his sidestepping, and tire flips, which were followed by a burpee after each rep. All of this translated into a high level of stiffness and soreness at the end of each day, so we also had Donald use our in-house compression boots and cryotherapy chamber after he worked out. These were relatively obscure, high-tech instruments and unfamiliar even to Gary and me, but their effect on the recovery process was phenomenal. We were amazed at what just three minutes in the chamber could do to flush out lactic acid and improve his circulation and flexibility.

Donald has taken the GLS philosophy like a fish to water and has been building his own workouts to prepare for SMU's training camp. Despite all the excitement, he's managed to maintain a clear vision, and to stay patient, confident, and relaxed as the summer approaches. It wasn't that long ago that he was playing football for fun, rather than looking at it as a potential career. He's gained a lot of perspective on the importance of avoiding injury.

"A lot of people, unfortunately, they're going to learn the hard way," he says. "If you can't stay on the field, it's the next man up. It's a cold business, but that's how it operates."

To keep up his energy for three workouts a day, Donald is especially mindful about maintaining proper diet and sleep schedules, and while he never shies away from a new challenge, he's also careful to avoid putting himself under too much stress. Donald's positive attitude, attention to detail, and willingness to ask questions and learn have made him an extraordinary role model for younger players. Donald Clay has been an enormous source of pride for us at GLS Training Facility.

Slant Board Flow Series

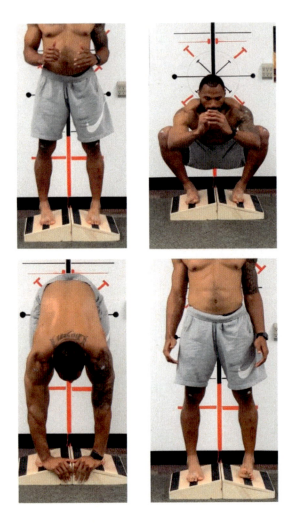

Fine tune the ball and socket systems in the body

Slant Board Double Drop

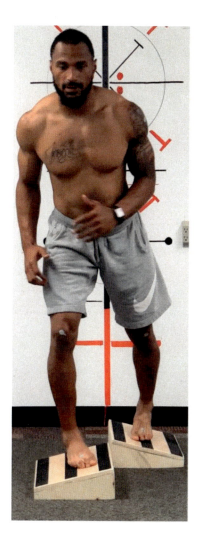

Fine tune the ball and socket systems in the body

Wall Drop In

Fine tune the ball and socket systems in the body

5. Drills and Exercises for GOATA Strength

Front Bar Squat

For decades barbell squats have been an essential tool for athletes in the weight room. In addition to improving range of motion, building the quads, calves, and hamstrings and strengthening the ligaments and connective tissues that give the lower body structure and balance these exercises also offer all the advantages of anaerobic training which improves the body's ability to access energy from fat. With all these benefits, it's a shame that squats have led to so many hip, knee, and back injuries, most of which are attributable to improper form: standing with duck feet, collapsing the legs inward, lifting heels off the ground, allowing the knees to bend in front of the toes, and so forth.

What I like about front bar squats is how they tend to take many of these mistakes out of the equation. If you grip the perpendicular handlebars you're unlikely to draw your shoulders into your chest, lean too far over your feet, or hunch your back over as if you were doing a good-morning or a deadlift. This is a quintessentially back-chain dominant exercise and rather than working the lumbar spine—which was never the point of an effective squat anyway—the real work is done by the haunches and hip abductors.

The head should be up, the neck should be comfortable and the feet should be planted about a shoulder-width apart. You'll know the bar is at an appropriate height if you can lift it off the rack by straightening your torso and pushing off with your legs, though it shouldn't be necessary to stand on your toes. To keep your form clean, it can be helpful to work with mirrors, or an attentive spotter since you won't want to look down once you begin to bend your knees. But an even better indicator should be your own back: if you can't keep your spine long and strong without the use of a belt, then the weight is too heavy.

Other signs that you should reduce the load are buckling in the knees or quivering in the ankles. Squats after all, are as much about working stabilizer muscles as they are about building the leg muscles that are already big and strong so that once you start to drop in, the movement is smooth and controlled. The rear end should be sticking out and the knees should flex outwards moving at the classic 22.5 degrees away from the navel and either the big toe or second toe of each foot should face directly forward. Continue to keep your eyes up and lower the bar until your legs are bent at an angle slightly sharper than 90 degrees. Remember to breathe deeply and explode upwards—pushing off from the fourth or fifth metatarsals and the outside of the heels. Continue to straighten your legs until you are standing normally, and then activate the glutes, which should be doing almost as much work as the quads. The back, by comparison, should feel little or no fatigue no matter how many reps you do.

Wishbone Squat

As I mentioned earlier in the book, the biggest shortcoming of most weightlifting regimens is that they tend to restrict motion to one single direction or vector. The pushes, pulls, dips, raises, presses, and rows of a traditional routine are great for subjecting individual muscles to extraordinary levels of stress. This is part of the reason why they're so popular since the muscles swell up in response. Athletes look stronger even if the training doesn't necessarily prepare them for anything besides bodybuilding. If you're looking for success in any other sport then it's probably worth thinking about how you move in three dimensions, instead of just two.

This is why I've advocated modifications to conventional squats. Though these exercises offer a lot of potential benefits for hockey, lacrosse, gymnastics, and track and field, they're particularly sought after to improve a football player's tackle, a wrestler's leg attack, or other techniques that involve moving someone of similar size and weight off of their center of gravity. In order to execute them properly you need to be able to move the weight both vertically and horizontally—starting very low, and driving with the forefoot as well as possibly also lifting the heels off the ground—all of which can be hard to safely recreate with a freestanding barbell that's been loaded with plates. Moreover, by setting up the movement of the weight on a static hook or axle (sometimes called a landmine station) you can transfer a lot of the stress on your knees and back directly onto the lower body muscles you're trying to develop.

If you have access to one of these machines my advice is to take advantage of it. They're great for calf raises or overhead presses (both discussed below) but I often have clients use them for an exercise that combines a calf raise with a squat. Start by finding a comfortable height for the shoulder pads then checking your posture, bending your knees, and sticking out your rear end as you drop in.

In the same way that an archer's bow string gathers energy as the arrow is pulled back, your legs should gather energy as your knees bend. As always, it's important to make sure your toes point forward and the inside ankle bones stay high, all while having the knees flex outward at 22.5 degrees away from the navel. When your thighs go past the 90-degree point relative to your calves, explode back up to a standing position while also keeping in mind to breathe.

You'll know you're doing it right if you can feel the weight move from the outside of the midfoot to the balls of your feet as you corner and extend your legs. In fact, it's not necessarily a mistake for your feet to rotate especially if you move directly from the squat into a calf raise. If you do this, then once you're at the highest point of the movement, your heels should both stick outwards and away from the tailbone. Even if both of your feet are parallel and facing forward the effect should make you look slightly pigeon toed.

Calf Raises

The trap bar is a highly underrated piece of weightlifting equipment. It's fantastic for doing deadlifts, farmer's walks, and even rows or chest presses, but it also allows you to do calf raises while avoiding many of the risks associated with conventional barbells. To begin with bearing the weight with your hands requires less skill than holding it on your shoulders. It's also safer: the plates are closer to the ground and less likely to slip or fall and compared to a straight bar, your posture is all but guaranteed to be more upright. With a trap bar the locked-leg position of a calf raise is less likely to hurt your knees and of course, the possibility of lower back damage is significantly reduced. Lower stress on your joints means you'll be able to recover from each set faster and ultimately, complete more reps.

When I supervise clients doing trap bar calf raises in the gym, I watch to see how they shift from the heel or midfoot up to the toes as they resist the pull of gravity. This may appear to happen along a single plane but if you're doing everything correctly you should still feel like you're transferring energy *past* and *around* the pivot points on both feet. Even though you're only lifting the weight a few inches it's a mistake to think of this as a two-dimensional movement. On the contrary, clients who have really started to master trap bar calf raises tend to incorporate an actual spin into them so that if they start with the toes pointed slightly outwards, and they should start to point inwards as they begin to move. At the high point the calves in both legs should be fully contracted, and the heels should jut out and away from the tailbone. Then, while the client lowers the weight, the feet should rotate back to their original position.

Training this way also harnesses the maximum benefit of calf raises for athletes. As we all know, doing these regularly with a trap bar tends to make the calf muscles a little prettier but it also helps to build the stabilizing muscles we rely on for running, jumping, skating, or cycling, as well as during plyometric exercises such as ladder drills or box jumps. Moreover, trap bar calf raises can help safeguard against injuries by making your lower legs more resistant to a sudden impact or unexpected torque which is why they're so useful for the side-step movements of basketball, soccer, or hockey.

Sorinex™ Hip Thrusts

It's hard to explain why so few strength and conditioning instructors don't include hip thrusts as a part of their training plans. The muscles involved in this exercise are essential to the fast-twitch movements of sports like football, lacrosse, and track and field and strengthening them can be especially helpful for runners and cyclists looking to build endurance. At the same time, front-chain dominant athletes who under-train their glutes and hamstrings, especially while overtraining the quads with leg presses or leg extensions—will often sacrifice flexibility and are that much more susceptible to knee and lower back problems. Even the upper body can be affected since building the muscles in the hips and rear end are important to stabilizing the movement of the chest and arms—as anyone who does tire flips, shot puts, or rock climbing will tell you.

Granted, one problem with hip thrusts is that it can be pretty uncomfortable to rest a dumbbell or a loaded barbell across the top of the thighs. Using individual plates instead is a little more practical but these can restrict your range of motion and unless you don't mind having an unwieldy stack of them on your lap it's difficult to make progress by increasing the load. With all this in mind, I've generally advocated the use of resistance bands since they don't involve any of the risks of lifting a static weight above your groin and also have the added advantage of reaching peak tension at the top of the movement when the hips are fully extended.

While at GLS Training Facility, I start work on the hip thruster by having clients rest their upper backs on a cushion. Depending on their preference clients may also want to rest their elbows on the cushion as well, which is not a problem. Once their feet are planted on the platform and they have the resistance band across their waist, they extend their pelvis upwards, until the body forms something like a plank. Many instructors suggest activating the core muscles but a better suggestion would be to pay attention to the cornering in the hips so that when the glutes are fully contracted the user should feel their knees pivoting inwards.

It's also OK to lift your heels off the ground, as you would with a wishbone squat. In this case you should also feel a pivoting from your midfoot to the fourth or fifth metatarsals and you may end up rotating your feet from a slightly duck-footed position, to a pigeon-toed position. The main thing to remember though, is that this exercise is not primarily for the legs or lumbar spine. (If you look on Instagram, you'll find several people making this oversight, especially when they start adding crazy amounts of resistance or weight.) To keep the focus on the glutes, check with a mirror or training partner to ensure that your back remains neutral. If it starts to arch, or if your quads are flexed, then it might be worth lowering the resistance or removing it entirely until you've corrected your form.

Vertical Climber

The vertical climber we use at GLS might remind clients of gyms from the 1980s. These machines were once as common as treadmills or stationary bikes and though they're no longer as popular their advantages have ceased to go away; in the twenty-first century coaches and rehab therapists have continued to recommend them for circuit training and low impact cardio workouts that unlock the spine and strengthen the core. They're great for developing the smooth contralateral movement that athletes need, and they can do a great deal to build the neuromuscular habits that help stave off knee problems and lower back pain. As it happens, these are the same essential habits I've mentioned earlier when describing the natural grace and fluidity of a baby's crawl, and I tend to bring them up again when clients place their feet on a vertical climber's footpads, grip the handlebars, and get ready to move.

The head should be up, the neck and shoulders should be relaxed, the rear end should stick slightly out, the inside ankle bones should be high, and the back should feel long and strong. I try to make sure the hips are open and loose and allow for a gentle side-to-side movement—never exaggerated but always there—as the client begins to engage the three main locomotive engines in the shoulders, hips, and lumbar spine. As the right hand pushes the grip upwards and the right knee pushes downwards, the upper torso should shift over the left side of the body. Once the right leg is fully extended, the left hip should be drawn back, the left knee should be flexed outwards from the hip, and the right shoulder should be shifted forward—all at about 22.5 degrees. At that point of course, the process repeats itself in the opposite direction until the left leg is fully extended and the left hand is fully raised while the left shoulder is shifted forward, the right hip is drawn back, and the right knee is flexed

Powered By GOATA: Move Like the Greatest Of All Time Athletes

away from the hip—again, all at 22.5 degrees.

Perhaps the most important thing to remember is to keep the head over the hips. If you're doing this and emphasizing the cyclical, three-dimensional quality of the exercise, then you should experience a minimum of foot pain or knee pain and shin splints after using this machine. Instead, most of the fatigue should be in your quads, core, upper back, and calves—and possibly your lungs. In addition to the clear benefits to skeletal muscle, triathletes looking for a way to cross-train have seized on the vertical climber for versatile full body aerobic workouts that rival only what you can do with a rowing or elliptical machine. The results from interval training are particularly impressive. Even if you're not an endurance athlete if you're trying to enhance your flexibility, balance, and range of motion while also building stamina and speed, it's hard to think of a more powerful tool.

Side Bends

In many gyms, side bends using dumbbells or body weight are relegated to ab workouts. I suppose they can be useful for anyone looking to lose their love handles but in my opinion, this sells the exercise way short. Regardless of what they can do for your core muscles the real priority should be to strengthen and decompress the body's internal gyroscope located opposite the sternum where the upper and lower spinal cord meet. Though it's still a simple pack-and-release movement, if you're doing them properly and emphasizing coiling and rotation—side bends offer potential benefits to competitors in almost any sport you can name, from a golfer's swing to a wrestler's hip toss and from a swimmer's crawl to a soccer player's kick.

In my approach, clients begin side bends by standing with their feet about a hip socket-width apart, holding a sand bell, kettlebell, or barbell plate in either hand. As always, the head should rest directly above the hips and the chest should be open, the toes should point directly forward and the body weight should rest on the outside of the feet. As a client begins to draw one side of the rib cage to the near hip, allowing the barbell plate to slide down the thigh as the hand stretches towards the floor, I watch to make sure they keep their shoulders open and chest up. After reaching peak contraction in the oblique muscles on one side I have the client return to the original standing position, then shift to the other without stopping or holding the upper body in place. The next step is to spread the legs further apart which opens up the internal gyroscope even more, but the movement is basically the same: allow the plate to slide down the outside of each leg without letting the head or chest drop as the hand stretches down towards the floor. Once they've reached peak contraction on one side, they gently shift to the other—again, without stopping or otherwise bracing their core muscles.

Doing side bends regularly will improve flexibility in the spinal cord and can work wonders for reducing spasms or pain in the lower back. In addition to the obliques the exercise will strengthen the erector spinae, quadratus lumborum, and rectus muscles, as well as the smaller stabilizing muscles that work around and between the vertebrae. If executed properly, they will help prepare you for more complex movements, with heavier weight, and will do a great deal to prevent injuries.

Goblet Squat

Like the front squat, goblet squats allow you to access all the benefits of traditional back squats all while removing most of the risks. You'll still be able to strengthen your quads, calves, glutes, and hamstrings, enhance movement integrity and balance, and do more to challenge the stabilizing muscles in your hips than you ever could on a leg press machine. At the same time, keeping your chest upright and your shoulders open during goblet squats doesn't take an extraordinary amount of technical prowess or skill. They're easy to do right; in other words, you won't need a lot of instruction to keep a stable S-shape in your spine while preserving and building back-chain dominance in your lower body.

All of this starts with a comfortable stance, with the feet just slightly further than shoulder-width apart. To make sure the work is done by the haunches and hip abductors rather than the lower back—the key thing to remember is to maintain the posture of the upper body as you bend your legs. To make sure the head and chest are upright, and the shoulders are never drawn too far in, it helps to grab the kettlebell by the horns and hold it fairly close to the sternum. As with other squats the feet should be pointed directly forward and during the drop-in, you should feel the weight shift between the fourth or fifth metatarsals and the outside of the heels.

The magic of this movement is in the ankles. To enforce proper cornering, I sometimes have clients do goblet squats with slant boards but it's perfectly safe to do these with the feet on an unbiased surface so long as there are no signs of pain or fatigue in the lower back after a given set. As always, the rear end should be sticking slightly out—with a bit of experience, it should come within just a few inches off of the floor—and the knees should flex outwards about 22.5 degrees away from the navel while the elbows brush the insides of each leg. Even if you're not that flexible the low point of this movement should feel like the loading of a spring, after which you should explode upwards feeling a natural shift in the weight from your heels and midfoot to the balls of your feet.

At lower weights, goblet squats are a particularly good fit for workouts geared towards elevating the heart rate and building lean muscle. By all means, it's possible to imagine some people use these as an anaerobic exercises for basic strength training, but more often than not, they make up a part of a circuit routine along with other full-body movements that are better-suited for building stamina than simply getting bigger or stronger. Naturally you'll do plenty to enhance lactic acid resistance in your lower body and are almost guaranteed to feel a burn in your quads and calves after a long set. It's not a bad sign if your core muscles are fatigued too, and given the unique handle on the kettlebell, this version of squatting can do a lot to challenge your grip.

Sand bell Squat

Sand bell squats are even safer than wishbone or front bar squats and can do even more for your balance and grip than goblet squats. For these reasons, they're ideal for newer clients or people who feel awkward or uncomfortable with more conventional versions of the same movement. The basic purpose however, is the same: done properly, sand bell squats will improve your range of motion and build muscles in the lower body that are responsible for durable elasticity while also safeguarding against injury from overuse or sudden torque.

As always, it's crucial that the work is being done by the quads, hamstrings, glutes, and calves, and not by the lower back. I have clients adopt the same stance as with other squats, with the feet facing forward and slightly more than shoulder-width apart, and while also reminding them to keep the chest and chin facing up and outwards and ensuring that the upper back is never hunched over. There are lots of options for how you grip the sand bell—and more advanced practitioners can actually alternate holding it between the left and right hand for each rep—but for beginners it probably makes the most sense to fold the forearms over each other into an X-shape, securing the sand bell in place against the chest. This puts you into the best possible position when you begin to bend your legs, since you're unlikely to hunch your shoulders or lean too far over your feet even if you're really giving the sand bell a tight hug. From here, the sequence should be pretty familiar. The rear end should stick out slightly, and during a drop-in, it's worth imagining the weight shifting *past* and *around* your ankles and hips so that once you've reached the low point of the exercise it should be fully concentrated on either the midfoot or heel. Again, like the string of an archer's bow, the legs should feel as if they're gathering energy as the knees bend at the classic 22.5-degree angle away from the navel. The next step is to release that energy as you launch upward keeping the head over the feet and the shoulders stable.

Many coaches have suggested variations for sand bell squats by incorporating two-handed curls or overhead presses into the exercise. The idea is to create a full-body exercise that will challenge the stabilizing muscles in the arms and torso; I don't object to this in theory but before making any additions to the movement it's extremely important to make sure you're properly engaging your hips and ankles since these are the parts of your body you'll depend on the most when traveling through space. By concentrating on the basics you're likely to draw the greatest possible benefits from sand bell squats over time.

Squat Series for Compressing Explosives

Bilateral loading to create strength

Wishbone Calf Raise

Bilateral loading to create strength

Powered By GOATA: Move Like the Greatest Of All Time Athletes

Front Bar Series for Balance, Crawling or Coiling Explosives

Bilateral loading to create strength

Calf Series for Foot Explosives

Bilateral loading to create strength

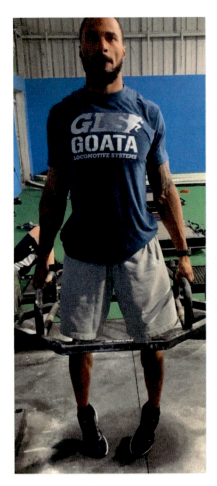

6. Drills and Exercises for GOATA Fluidity

Weck Club Swings

At some point in our lives, almost everyone has witnessed the way one side of their body can outwork or overpower the other. At GLS, I've come to rely on the Weck Rotational Movement Training Club—also called the RMT® Club—to help people overcome these imbalances, this has proven to be an extremely powerful tool. By working with this piece of equipment, clients can learn how to spot asymmetries that put a limit on one limb or one set of muscles and subject the more dominant side of the body to undue pressure. Exercising with the RMT Club can do wonders for anyone looking to develop a combination of strength, flexibility, and range of motion. By using it over time, as you begin to build power and balance in the upper body, you'll feel yourself engaging the hips and glutes more effectively too.

But what I really like about the RMT Club is the way it emphasizes coiling and spiraling in the shoulders, hips, and lower spine. This makes it far more useful than most barbells, dumbbells, or weight machines, which are built for simple movements in one direction and have limited application in the real world. If you're trying to improve the way you walk, run, jump, hit, strike, kick, or throw, it's crucial to see how these things are done in three dimensions.

The most basic exercise you can do with an RMT Club is more or less a figure-eight. I have clients start with a comfortable stance, in which the feet are parallel (a little more than shoulder-width apart) and the knees are slightly bent. If your left leg is in front, then you should start with your left palm down on the end of the club, and your right palm up, with the two hands an inch or two apart. To gather energy your head should be over your right foot, with your upper right arm tucked into the rib cage, and your right hip moved towards the navel. This is complemented by the position of the right shoulder which should shift slightly downwards and back.

At the start of the first arc, lead with the pinkie of the left hand and move the club as if hitting a golf ball off the tee. Straighten the arms as you swing the club towards the floor and then bend them as the club head rises back up, and straighten them again as the club head rises back up into the second arc. By this point the head should be over the left foot, the upper left arm should tuck back into the rib cage, and the left hip should shift down and away from the navel, guiding the club head to the high point on the other side of the body. Finally, straighten the arms as the club head descends for the second time, before it swings back up towards its original position. It's worth keeping in mind that the RMT Club is loaded with material that shifts inside the core of the club head, creating a form of dynamic resistance that you can feel (and hear) if you suddenly change direction.

As with any other low-weight exercise, Weck Club swings can make a fine addition to any circuit-style workout. They can be great for raising the heart rate, especially if you increase the speed and intensity, but before that happens my advice would be to make sure you've fully refined the movement on each side. After completing a set with your left leg in front, try to improve your symmetry by switching to the right and following the same series of steps.

Standing with Pro Pulsers

Arm movement is one of the most overlooked aspects of proper running form. Even if you've never thought about it, it's hard to keep our hips and lower back balanced when traveling through space without countering their rhythm with the shoulders, arms, and wrists. If you can improve the way you use your arms, you'll learn to gain speed and efficiency and prevent injury to the knees and feet by engaging proper weight distribution.

The first category of exercises I have clients do with these tools is called *bilateral* movement. For these, I have clients grip the pulsars so that the middle and ring finger make an "OK" sign around the second groove. The forefinger should go around the cap and the pinkie can go either underneath or around the side of the pulser. Clients can start with a *down-pulse*, holding the pulsars vertically at the hips, then move to a *push-pulse*, holding the pulsars horizontally, at about neck level, and finish with a *pull pulse*, lifting the elbows, and holding the pulsars vertically behind the neck, with the pinkies up. In each of these exercises, both hands should make an up-and-down pumping motion with the pulsars, keeping the hands in unison.

The second category is called *contralateral* movement and comes a little bit closer to the gathering and releasing of momentum that help enforce a better running form. To begin with, I have clients stand with their feet about two hand-widths apart, holding the pulsars vertically, and pump the arms as if running in place, but without moving the lower body. The next step is to get into more of a runner's stance; though the arm movement is the same, one foot should be a stride-length in front of the other, and the toes of both feet should point slightly towards the navel, which will help the inside ankle bones stay high. Once you've gotten into this stance, try to keep the head over the front hip, syncing the movement of each pulser with the side-to-side shifting of your body weight, then move your head over the back hip, and do several more reps. Repeat the movement with your other foot in front, taking the same pigeon-toed stance, and starting with your head over your front hip before moving to the back.

Rope Tether Ball Swings

Another way to learn effective coiling involves swinging a medicine ball attached to a sturdy length of rope. The gear is fairly simple and hard to break and it doesn't take me long to teach clients to use this equipment for introductory movements, like figure-eights. Over time, you'll be able to translate the spiraling of your hands into a balanced, complementary cycling engine in your arms, hips, and legs. This is enormously useful to athletes, and you'd be surprised at the number of complex variations that are possible once you've mastered the basics.

All of this starts with how you position your grip. A few versions of the rope-and-medicine-ball involve a smaller cord-lock or bead at the end of the rope, which prevents the gear from slipping out of the user's hands, but it's fine to simply tie two knots, leaving enough space between them to fit two closed fists. You'll want to be able to stack the pinkie of one hand on top of the thumb of the other and then rotate them in a wide helix, resisting the temptation to simply shift your wrists from side to side. To make sure you're ready, it's not a bad idea to rehearse the movement for a few cycles without anything in your hands.

Moreover, once you're holding the rope, you'll want to start slow. One foot should be about a stride-length in front of the other, your toes should face forward, your knees should be slightly bent, and your glutes and lower back should be activated, but not tense. As you begin to move the ball through the air, the goal should be to guide it through an exaggerated figure-eight so that its path will ultimately form two large circles on either side of your body. When the movement starts to feel smooth and comfortable, pick up the pace, allowing the rope to run through the widest-possible arcs.

Beginners should aim to do it for 30-second intervals, and eventually try out some variations. You can add weight and slow the cadence to work on strength or reduce the weight and speed things up to work on explosivity. Keeping the arm straight, discus throwers can try holding the rope with one hand and rotating with the arc of the ball parallel to the floor. Bowlers meanwhile, can derive a lot of benefit from rotating either shoulder in broad vertical circles. This in turn, can be developed into a "pulser swing," adding a horizontal push-and-pull action to the movement which converts the circular path of the ball into more of an ellipse. Some of these take longer to learn than others, and you may feel your abs burning after several intervals, but the biggest benefits are to the three major coiling engines that GOATAs rely on, which are the shoulders, the lower spine, and the hips.

Traveling and Fluidity Up-leveling Series

Wind and whip the energy with devices

Rope and RMT Swing Series for Fluidity

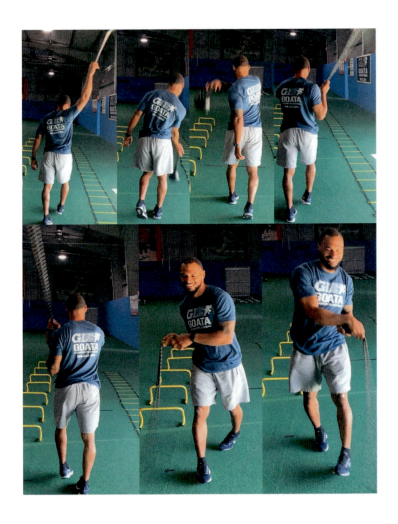

Weck RMT whip swing

7. Drills and Exercises for GOATA Explosivity

BOSU® Ball Squats with Plyo Box

If you've visited a contemporary gym at any time in the past fifteen years, you've noticed that plyo boxes are trending. Plyometric exercises can be a fantastic warm-up for the lower body and while they do a great deal to strengthen the quads, glutes, hamstrings, and calves—just as much work is being done by the smaller stabilizing muscles in the hips as well. To nail this point home, I like to use a BOSU® Balance Trainer, another superb invention of David Weck's, which is always helpful for enforcing smart, purposeful movement (if used correctly!). Make sure the box you're using is wide enough to support the surface area of the BOSU ball's base. Assuming the box is well-constructed, it's unlikely that either piece of equipment will move but it never hurts to use a textured high friction tape to prevent slipping or sliding which can lead to a fall. Once the BOSU ball is in position, stand on it with the feet a hip socket-width apart and hold the resistance band with both fists, gripping it as you would a baseball bat. Gather energy by bending into a squat with your rear end extending slightly outwards, then straighten your legs until you're standing again. After several reps, release the resistance band, swing the arms back, and launch the feet up and off the BOSU ball, while remembering to corner properly in the ankles and knees so that your heels both jut away from the tailbone.

While these can be a great cardio exercise in longer sets, it will sometimes be tempting to rush through them. There's nothing wrong with picking up the pace for these, especially if you've integrated them into a circuit routine, but doing so on the first or second workout is probably a mistake. Pay attention to how you stand on the ball, enforce a symmetrical pose, and watch to make sure that the soles of both feet are hitting the ground at the same time.

High Knee Skipping with Pro Pulsars

While Pro Pulsars can do wonders as a strength tool, they're even more impressive for building explosivity. If you feel comfortable with the *bilateral* and *contralateral* versions of the exercises, the next logical step is to find a straightaway on the sidewalk or track—at GLS, we use a 50-yard section of astroturf—and try them out while traveling through space, incorporating a bounding stride or a skip.

These are not unlike a cherry-picking cardio drill, in which a knee launches into the air just as the opposite hand is raised. With the pulsars, the result should feel very similar to the series of movements you did when standing still since the coiling of the hips, lower spine, and shoulders are still being complemented by the shifting of the weight in the pulsars. If you're doing it right, the inside material will hit the bottom of the left-hand pulsar at about the same time as the left foot leaves the ground, and the material on the right-hand pulsar should hit the bottom at the same time as the launching of the right foot. You can make things more challenging by either extending each hand higher into the air or by pulling either knee higher into the chest.

Using the hand pulsars regularly, you should find yourself learning to run "taller"—with a longer, stronger spine. You'll get more power out of each step and it will be much easier to notice and correct inefficiencies resulting from duck feet or low inside ankle bones—which push the body sideways, instead of forward. It may be hard to believe that anyone could actually run faster while holding a pair of weights, but you may eventually feel as though the hand pulsars give you an unfair advantage. As you get more comfortable, holding them will be a little like grasping a pair of rails, which you can pull and push off to gain stability and momentum.

Landmine Presses

There are lots of ways a landmine station can be used for challenging three-dimensional movements that put relatively low impact on the joints. The advantages of this bar-and-axle setup are particularly prominent in landmine presses, which is an exercise that brings both the upper and lower body into play, but also poses a minimal risk to the connective tissue in the shoulders or lower back.

After loading the plates, I have clients get into a staggered stance, with the toes of both feet facing forward. You should be far enough from the axle so that when the arms are flexed, the end of the bar will comfortably touch the chest, though not so close that you lose balance when the arms are fully extended. Once you're in a comfortable position, hold the top of the bar with the same side hand as the front leg, with the other hand directly under it.

The movement is a little bit like throwing a shot putter's ball, but without any elaborate wind-up. During the *drop-in*, as you lower the bar, the front knee should bend outwards, away from the navel, while the back hip should rotate inwards, both at 22.5 degrees. The chest should complement this movement, so that the front shoulder also rotates downwards and back—again, at 22.5 degrees towards the navel—until you're fully coiled. Then, during the *cornering* phase, you should feel the energy moving from the heels to the fourth or fifth metatarsals of either foot, letting the hips lead as you push the bar away. After fully straightening the arms, the *release* should feel smooth and controlled, so that the axle rotates along approximately the same plane with each rep. After you've completed a full set, you'll want to switch the stance, reverse the position of both hands, and repeat the same classic steps on the other side of the body: *drop-in, cornering,* and *release.*

You'll obviously feel most of the fatigue in your chest and shoulders, though it's important to remember that this is not just a tricked-out version of an overhead press. To begin with, because so much friction is being transferred to the base of the axle, the risk of injuring your rotator cuff is significantly less than any exercise in which two dumbbells—or even the grips of a weight machine, are pushed above the ears. Instead, almost all the work is being done by the muscle groups in your back and hips, which are made to naturally coil and uncoil as you push the bar into the air. If you're doing everything correctly this will feel like a metal spring being wound up, and then released.

Front Bar Side Bend Squat One-legged Lifts

Explode the 22.5 indicators

Powered By GOATA: Move Like the Greatest Of All Time Athletes

Pulsing Series for Explosives Featuring Weck Method Pro Pulsars

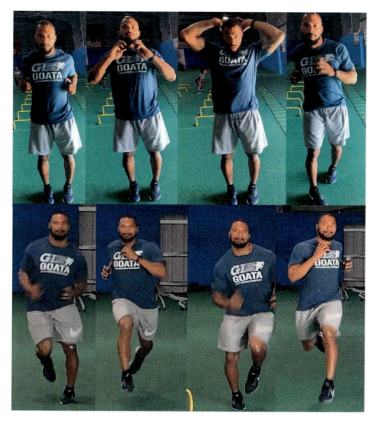

Use the strong side of your hand to create explosives

8. Advice for Athletes

In all my years as an athlete, trainer, and coach, I've never *seen* the fitness profession move at a faster pace than it does today. Not only is the recovery industry booming with innovations like cryotherapy, percussive therapy, stem cell infusion, and myofascial release, but the market is now overrun with experts in healing modalities like deep tissue massage, rolfing, trigger point therapy, and proprioceptive neuromuscular facilitation. The formal study of sports medicine is an equally crowded field and if you visit any decent library you're likely to find the subject covered in over 100 peer-reviewed journals in English alone. Most of these are published on a quarterly or monthly basis and what's printed in April will often contradict what was printed in March. If you're plugged into the academic or the commercial side of things you may get the impression that only the latest studies are worth paying attention to and that unless you have access to the most up-to-date technology, you're wasting your time. I've read a great deal from these academic journals, and I follow the recovery business closely. This is my passion after all, and yet I sometimes worry that by keeping up with the science of sport, people lose sight of the big picture. Decades after universities first started offering advanced degrees in kinesiology, and millions of Americans poured into aerobics and bodybuilding gyms, the most useful insights from the profession remain more or less the same: get plenty of rest, manage stress and anxiety, pursue a balanced diet, and try to stay in motion.

If you prioritize nutrition, sleep, and quality movement, then everything else will fall into place. No one is safe from the aging process—Father Time always wins—but every one of us has the ability to preserve the soft tissue and cartilage between the knees, hip sockets, and vertebrae that help us stay pain-free, whether we're throwing a ball, riding a bike, swimming in a pool, or enjoying a walk in the park. Every day, new coaching methods and recovery tools are coming out that offer a new way to avoid sudden injuries or repetitive damage but in my opinion, success will ultimately come to those who recognize the assets they were

Powered By GOATA: Move Like the Greatest Of All Time Athletes

born with and are willing to work to keep them. In other words, the best way to prevent muscle atrophy, brittle bones, and a loss of metabolism is simply to keep moving.

As I said before, no one understands this better than kids. Before they've spent hours working at a desk, sitting behind a steering wheel, or watching Netflix on the couch, young children seem to instinctively know that by staying in forward motion they can keep their muscles healthy and flexible. This is fundamental to overcoming the effects of a sedentary lifestyle and yet it sometimes feels as though the fitness industry is built on denying it, establishing shortcuts and machines which are likely to backfire or to pose hazards that can be greater than the benefits. As exciting as all this new technology can be, from experience, I've learned that the clearest route to recovery is to try to learn high quality movement from the beginning.

And it's never too late to form these habits. If you've only just started going to a gym regularly or if the ideas I've laid out in this book sound new and unfamiliar, my advice is to be patient. Muscle and soft tissue need time to adapt and regenerate to any new form of stress, and the most carefully-designed fitness plan can still fall apart if you move too quickly. (Think of your body as if it were an old, out-of-tune piano: rush the process of tightening the strings, they're liable to pop.) Regardless of age, I guarantee that your work on alignment and posture will pay off if you're consistent. Even if you don't have a slow-motion camera, try and take note of the movement brilliance of a few GOATAs, and pretty soon, you'll find yourself feeling less pain, sustaining fewer injuries, and getting more fun out of life. You don't have to be a serious athlete. Just get out there and play.

Mentors

David Weck

Kelly Starrett

Eric Goodman & Brian King

Mentors are needed to coach greatness!!

GOATA Bow

GOATA Bow = absorb and load energy

GOATA Shape

GOATA Shape: perfect the columns by perfecting the lines and levels

GOATA 22.5° Drop-In

Endurance durability: let the movement quality keep you durable

Heel Away, Elbow Way

If you walk like a champ, then you can strike, swing, run, jump, hit, throw, and kick like a champ.

Heel Away On Release

The secrets are in the toddlers

Jose G Boesch

Stand Up Crawling is Running and Walking

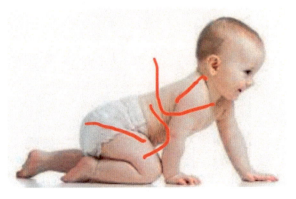

Let the toddlers show you the way

Elbow Away

Heel Away

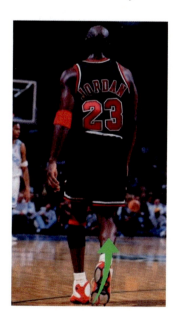

GOATA: The simplest way to have endurance durable connective tissue security, and explosive fluid movement ever discovered by watching super athletes and babies. No bio-medical gobbledygook, spiritual woo woo, or fitness mumbo jumbo needed.

Made in the USA
Monee, IL
25 July 2020

36948353R00062